SNAKES AND LIZARDS

Anne Smith

Nature Study

Bees and Wasps
Frogs and Toads
Rabbits and Hares
Snakes and Lizards
Spiders
Worms

All photographs from Oxford Scientific Films

Editor: Joanne Jessop

First published in 1989 by
Wayland (Publishers) Limited
61 Western Road, Hove
East Sussex, BN3 1JD, England

Originally published in 1985 as
Discovering Snakes and Lizards
by Neil Curtis

British Library Cataloguing in Publication Data
Smith, Anne
    Snakes and lizards.
    1. Lizards   2. Snakes
    I. Title   II. Series
    597.95

ISBN 1–85210–766–9

Typeset by Kalligraphics Ltd, Horley, Surrey.
Printed in Italy by G.Canale and C.S.p.A, Turin.
Bound in France by A.G.M.

Cover: The green palm viper lives in the tropical rain forest of Costa Rica in Central America.
Frontispiece: This boldly patterned snake is an adder.

Contents

Words that appear in **bold** in the text are explained in the glossary.

Introducing snakes and lizards

Snakes and lizards are **reptiles**. Reptiles are cold-blooded animals. This means that the sun's heat warms their bodies. If the weather is warm, a reptile feels warm. If the weather is cool, then it feels cool.

➡ An iguana is a kind of lizard. It lives in the trees of tropical jungles.

➤ The diamondback rattlesnake lives in Texas.

Because they need the heat of the sun to warm their bodies, most snakes and lizards live in warmer parts of the world. Those that live in cooler countries **hibernate** during the winter.

Snakes and lizards are usually long and thin. Most lizards have four legs, but snakes have no legs.

Both snakes and lizards are covered with **scales** and their skin is almost waterproof. Snakes and lizards never sweat.

The history of snakes and lizards

Dinosaurs were reptiles that lived millions of years ago. Dinosaur bones have been found in rocks. These bones are called **fossils**. We know from these fossils that dinosaurs, snakes and lizards probably had the same **ancestors**.

▲ This land iguana looks like a dinosaur.

▼ Staurikosaurus was a kind of dinosaur.

There were many different kinds of dinosaurs. Some were very big, and others were very small. Some ate plants, and some ate other dinosaurs.

Some lizards look rather like dinosaurs, but they walk in a different way. This is because a lizard's legs are on the side of its body. A dinosaur's legs were under its body. Some dinosaurs walked and ran on their hind legs only.

➡ This chart shows the history of reptiles and birds. Lizards first appeared about 200 million years ago. Snakes came later, about 136 million years ago.

At Present	Turtles	Snakes	Lizards	Crocodiles	Birds
Previous Ages (millions of years ago)					
Cenozoic					
— (65) —					Pteranodon
Cretaceous				Triceratops	
—(136)—			Brontosaurus		
Jurassic					Ichthyosaurus Plesiosaurus
—(193)—					
Triassic					
—(225)—		Euparkeria			
Permian					
—(280)—					
Carboniferous					

What snakes and lizards look like

What snakes look like

Snakes have no legs. The shortest snake is about 10 cm long. Snakes such as pythons and anacondas may be up to 9 m long.
Snakes have scales all over their bodies. The scales help them to move along the ground. Some snakes move by bending their bodies, like waves pressing against the ground.

➡ A rattlesnake flicking out its tongue. It is looking for food.

A snake can open its mouth very wide. This means it can swallow food that is bigger than its own head.

A snake has no ear openings and its eyes do not have eyelids.

↟ Each kind of snake has a different pattern of scales. These are a python's scales.

The Skull of a Snake

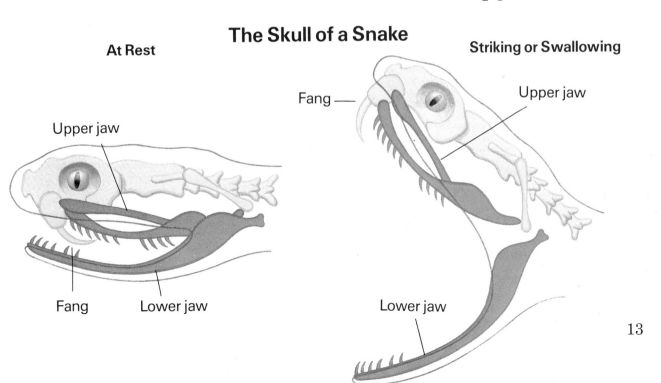

At Rest

Upper jaw

Fang   Lower jaw

Striking or Swallowing

Fang —

Upper jaw

Lower jaw

13

What lizards look like

The smallest lizard is about 5 cm long. The giant Komodo dragon may be up to 3 m long.

➤ Look for the lizard's ear opening and its simple teeth.

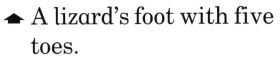

➤ A lizard's foot with five toes.

➤ This lizard has lost its tail. But it will grow a new one.

A lizard's skin is tough and covered with rows of scales. Between the scales is soft skin that helps the lizard to move its body easily. Scales stop the lizard from drying up. They also protect the lizard.

A lizard has ear openings on its head, and it has simple teeth. Its eyes are protected by eyelids.

Most lizards have four legs, with five toes on each foot. Each toe has a claw.

If an enemy catches a lizard by the tail, it will break off. This lets the lizard escape. The lizard will grow a new tail.

Where snakes and lizards live

On land

Most snakes and lizards live on land. They are found in almost every country of the world.

➨ This snake lives in the rain forest. It can also climb trees.

▲ Some snakes like to live near water. This grass snake is shedding its skin.

Many snakes and lizards are good swimmers and spend a lot of time in the water. Others like to live near rivers and ponds. There are some snakes that live in muddy swamps and feed on small fish. Some snakes and lizards can climb trees and steal baby birds from nests. Some can even glide through the air from tree to tree.

Snakes and lizards live wherever they can find food. Some live in woods and forests, some live on hillsides, and some live in deserts. A few even live in houses. Because snakes have long, thin bodies, they can slide into cracks in walls.

➤ This gecko lizard lives in the desert. It digs into the sand to escape the heat.

In the sea

The marine iguana is the only kind of lizard that feeds in the sea. It lives on the Galapagos Islands off the west coast of South America. The marine iguana lies on rocks in the warm sunshine and then dives into the cold sea to feed on seaweed. It can swim well, but it has to come to the surface to breathe.

← This sea snake is very poisonous.

The sea snake spends most of its time in the sea. It feeds on fish, and stays under water for a long time. The flat shape of its body helps it to move quickly through the water.

◀ A marine iguana feeds under water on seaweed.

19

Food and feeding

Finding food

Many snakes shoot out their tongues to 'taste' the air. This is how they find out if food is nearby.

Pit vipers are snakes that hunt in the dark. They have pits on their heads that can feel the warmth of any animal that is nearby.

Snakes have no ears to hear with. They feel movements in the ground through their bodies.

Most lizards use their eyes to find their **prey**.

A rattlesnake 'tastes' the ◗ air with its tongue.

The chameleon is a lizard that lives in trees. Its eyes can move in different directions. A chameleon can see forwards and backwards at the same time. When it spots an insect, it shoots out its sticky tongue to catch it.

➤ The chameleon has a very long sticky tongue.

Different kinds of food

Lizards and snakes eat many different kinds of food. Small lizards eat mainly insects. Larger lizards eat plants or small animals. The poisonous gila monster eats other reptiles and birds' eggs. The giant Komodo dragon eats animals as big as deer and wild pigs.

➤ Small lizards eat insects. This gecko has caught a moth.

⬆ Komodo dragons are the largest lizards on earth. They eat large animals.

➡ This snake is burrowing into a termite nest.

Snakes that burrow under the ground usually eat worms and ants. Other snakes eat lots of different kinds of animals, including birds, bats, frogs, toads, slugs and snails. Sea snakes eat small fish.

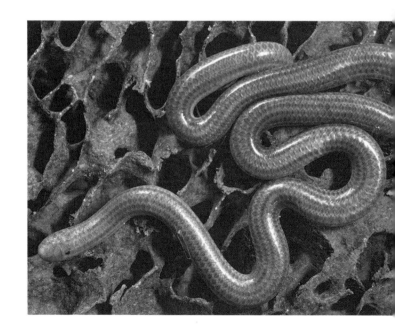

How snakes eat

Snakes have sharp teeth that point backwards. This helps them to grab and hold their prey. The snake then swallows its prey alive in one piece.

➡ This snake is eating a frog.

Some snakes are poisonous and can kill humans. They have **fangs** that inject poison into their prey. Some snakes spit **venom** into the eyes of their prey to blind it.

➤ A poisonous snake biting a lizard.

◆ A sand snake squeezing a lizard to death.

Pythons and boas are very large snakes. They are called constrictors. A constrictor winds its body around the prey and squeezes it to death. It then swallows its prey whole, head first.

Young snakes and lizards

Courtship and mating

Every year male and female snakes and lizards come together to **mate**.

When lizards are ready to mate, the male climbs on the female's back. He injects **sperm** into her body. The female's eggs are **fertilized** by the sperm. New reptiles will grow from these eggs.

▶ A male and female adder come together to mate.

Male

Female

Two lizards mating. The male is more colourful.

Before they mate, the male lizard dances around to attract the female. This is called **courtship**.

A male snake finds a female by following her scent. He rubs his chin against her and flicks his tongue over her body. He then winds his body around hers to mate.

Two iguanas courting.

Laying eggs

Female snakes and lizards do not lay many eggs, but the eggs are quite large. Each egg has a big yolk, which feeds the young as it develops inside the egg.

Most lizards dig a nest in which to lay their eggs. Snakes do not make nests. They lay their eggs among rocks or in piles of leaves. Most snakes and lizards leave their eggs after laying them. The eggs are kept warm by the sun.

➤ Grass snakes often lay their eggs on straw.

➤ This gecko has just hatched. It looks funny with a piece of shell on its head.

When it is ready to **hatch**, a young snake or lizard breaks the egg shell. It uses a sharp tooth called an 'egg tooth'. This tooth drops off soon after the young reptile has hatched.

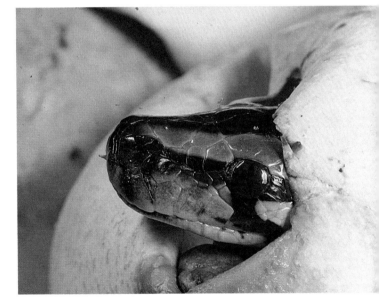

➤ You can see the egg tooth on this python.

From babies to adults

Most eggs take a few weeks to hatch. Snakes and lizards do not usually look after their babies once they have hatched.

Snakes and lizards grow very quickly. From time to time, they shed their skin. The new skin is soft and gives the young snakes and lizards more room to grow.

➡ Baby adders are much browner than their parents.

◆ A garden lizard sheds its old skin.

A snake sheds its skin in one piece. A lizard sheds its skin in many small pieces.

We do not know how long snakes and lizards live in the wild. When kept as pets, snakes can live for 30 years, and lizards for 20 years.

Living in a world of danger

Enemies of snakes and lizards

Many animals eat snakes and lizards. The African secretary bird even eats poisonous snakes. So do mongooses.

Humans kill the greatest number of snakes and lizards. People are often frightened of snakes and lizards, and if they see one they may try to kill it. Often the snakes and lizards that people kill are harmless.

◀ A mongoose family watching a puff adder.

This roadrunner has caught a lizard.

A grass snake pretends to be dead to trick an enemy.

Humans sometimes destroy the places where snakes and lizards live. People cut down forests. They drain swamps. They turn deserts into farmland. These are the places where snakes and lizards live.

Snakes that can kill

Most snakes will try to run away rather than attack an enemy. There are some snakes that can kill humans with a bite. These are vipers, cobras and sea snakes. Their poison is

➤ A black spitting cobra. It spits venom at its enemies.

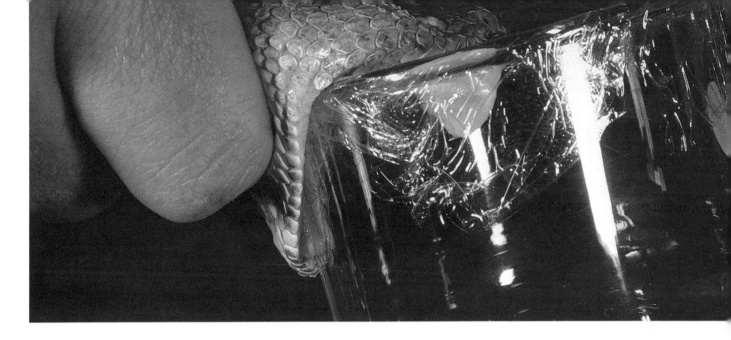

⬆ A tiger rattlesnake is made to spit venom into a jar. This is used to make anti-serum.

called venom. There are two main kinds of venom. One is nerve poison that may stop the **victim's** breathing or heartbeat. The other kind of snake venom poisons the victim's blood.

Snake bites are very dangerous. The medicine used to treat snake bites is called anti-serum. It is very hard to come by. A snake is made to bite into a piece of plastic over a jar. The venom falls into the jar. This is used to make anti-serum.

Camouflage

Animals do not want to be seen by their enemies. If the colour of an animal's body matches the place where it lives, it is difficult to see. This is called camouflage. It is used to trick the enemy.

➤ This Texan horned lizard is hard to see.

This snake's mottled skin makes a good camouflage.

The colouring of many snakes and lizards looks very much like the places where they live. It may be a green or brown **mottled** colour. Sometimes snakes and lizards are marked with stripes or patches of colour.

A chameleon can change the colour of two different parts of its body at once.

The long body of the horsewhip snake helps it to hide in trees.

Colours for display

Some snakes and lizards are very brightly coloured. Often the male lizard is brightly coloured to attract a female.

Poisonous snakes and a few poisonous lizards have bright bands or stripes of red, yellow or black. These bright colours warn their enemies to keep away.

➤ This bright coral snake can kill with its venom.

▲ This gila monster is a poisonous lizard. It lives in the USA and Mexico.

Sometimes a harmless snake has the same colouring as a poisonous snake. This is called mimicry. The bright colours warn an enemy to keep away even though the snake is not poisonous.

Protecting snakes and lizards

We can protect snakes and lizards by looking after the places where they live. This is called conservation.

Snakes and lizards may not seem very important. People often think of them as dangerous or unpleasant and want to kill them. But snakes and lizards can be very helpful to

➡ This picture shows some of the animals that feed on each other. These animals could all be poisoned if a farmer puts chemicals on his crops.

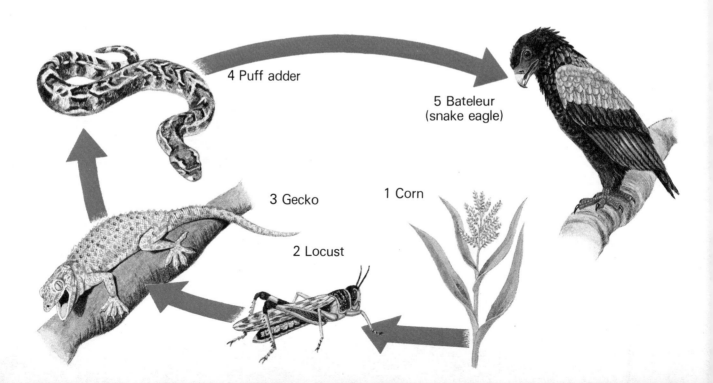

4 Puff adder

5 Bateleur
(snake eagle)

3 Gecko

1 Corn

2 Locust

humans. They eat insects that feed on farmers' crops. They are also food for other animals, such as the snake eagle. If we kill snakes and lizards, then the animals that feed on them will also die.

- Cutting down forests and jungles destroys the places where snakes and lizards live.

Learning more about snakes and lizards

In a terrarium

Many kinds of lizards make good pets. They need a home to live in called a terrarium. It is a wooden box with a glass front and a lid with air holes. A terrarium must be kept warm and dry.

A pet lizard will eat worms, insects or even minced meat. It will need fresh water every day to drink and to bathe in.

◀ This girl is holding a boa constrictor in a zoo.

It is not really a good idea to keep snakes as pets. They are difficult to keep because they need very special care.

You can learn more about snakes and lizards from books or by visiting a museum or zoo.

➡ A terrarium.

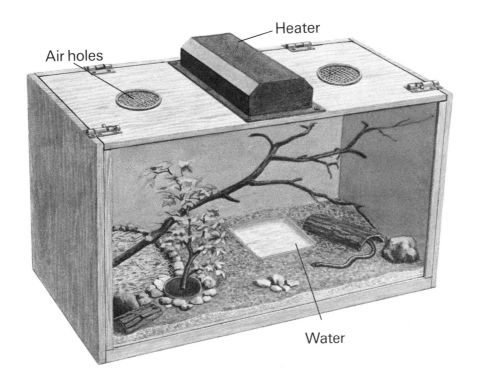

Air holes

Heater

Water

Out of doors

The best way to learn about animals is to study them out of doors, in the wild. Snakes and lizards are hard to find because they are shy animals. But you may find a snake's old skin. Snakes and lizards are most active on sunny days. They hide away in cold, wet weather.

◄ A slow-worm is a lizard that has no legs.

➤ A snake has just shed its old skin.

If you find where a snake or lizard lives, do not disturb it. If you are quiet and still, you may see it come out from its hiding place.

Remember that some snakes are poisonous. It is a good idea to wear shoes and long trousers in places where poisonous snakes might live.

Glossary

Ancestor An early type of animal from which later kinds of animals developed.

Courtship The behaviour of male and female animals before they mate.

Fang A long hollow tooth through which poisonous snakes inject venom into their prey.

Fertilized When sperm joins an egg, the egg is fertilized and begins to develop into a young animal.

Fossil Any animal remains, such as shell or a bone, preserved in rocks.

Hatch To break out of an egg.

Hibernate To sleep through the winter.

Mate To come together as male and female to produce young animals.

Mottled Marked with spots or patches.

Prey An animal that is killed and eaten by another animal.

Reptile A cold-blooded animal with a backbone and scaly skin. Snakes and lizards are reptiles.

Scales Small, thin bony plates that cover the bodies of reptiles and some fish.

Sperm A special fluid from the body of a male animal. It fertilizes the female's egg, which then develops into a young animal.

Venom The poisonous fluid produced by some snakes to harm or kill their enemies.

Victim An animal that is harmed or killed by another animal.

Finding Out More

If you would like to find out more about snakes and lizards, you could read the following books:

E. N. Arnold and J. A. Burton, *A Field Guide to the Reptiles and Amphibians of Britain and Europe* (Collins, 1978)
John Foden and Michael Sutton, *Reptiles* (Bartholomew, 1976)
T. Phelps, *Poisonous Snakes* (Blandford Press, 1981)
Donald Street, *Reptiles of Northern and Central Europe* (Batsford, 1979)
B. Stonehouse, *Venomous Snakes* (Wayland, 1981)
P. Whitfield, *Reptiles and Amphibians* (Longman, 1983)

Picture Acknowledgements

Survival Anglia – J. & D. Bartlett 23 (top); J. B. Davidson 21; J. Foott 27 (top); A. Root 34; S. Trevor 32. All other photographs from Oxford Scientific Films by the following photographers: G. I. Bernard *frontispiece,* 13, 14, 17, 24, 29 (bottom), 31, 33 (bottom), 35, 44 (top); J. A. L. Cooke 8, 9, 12, 15; (right), 20, 23 (bottom), 29 (top), 33 (top), 36, 37; S. Dalton 15 (left); F. Ehrenström 25 (top); M. Fogden *cover,* 25 (bottom), 38, 39; R. A. Lewin 42; Mantis Wildlife Films 27 (bottom); G. Merlen 10, 18; P. Parks 22; A. Ramage 44 (bottom); R. Redfern 30; P. K. Sharpe 16; D.Thompson 41; P. & W. Ward 19; G. J. Wren 28. Artwork by Wendy Meadway.

Index